THE
Boston
Tea Party

by RUSSELL FREEDMAN
illustrated by
PETER MALONE

Holiday House / New York

INTRODUCTION

ON THE NIGHT OF December 16, 1773, a band of colonists disguised as Mohawk Indians boarded three merchant ships that had arrived from Britain and anchored in Boston Harbor. Working quickly and silently, they hoisted thousands of pounds of tea up from the ships' holds and dumped the tea into the sea.

The Boston Tea Party was an act of defiance—a protest against the policies of the British Parliament and King George III, who ruled England's colonies in North America. Parliament had levied a tax on all tea shipped from England to America. The tax wasn't much, just three cents a pound, but it was the latest in a series of taxes that incited massive colonial opposition. The tax on tea was seen as a threat to the colonists' liberties and a symbol of British tyranny.

The colonists were British citizens, subjects of King George. They did not object to paying taxes, but they insisted that they should not be taxed by Parliament, a legislature an ocean away in which they had no voice. Their rallying cry was No taxation without representation! They demanded the right to raise all taxes

themselves, through their own elected representatives in their own colonial assemblies.

Americans enjoyed their tea. They gulped it down by the gallon. But they were willing to go without their favorite beverage rather than acknowledge Parliament's right to tax them. Throughout the thirteen colonies, they had agreed to boycott British tea. British tea ships were turned away from New York and Philadelphia and sent back to England with their unwanted cargoes. In Charleston, South Carolina, a shipment of tea that had been unloaded was stored in damp warehouse vaults and left to rot.

In Boston, where three tea ships were riding at anchor, the colonists were spurred to action. A group calling themselves the Sons of Liberty demanded that the ships leave Boston Harbor and carry their tea back to its English owners. But Thomas Hutchinson, the royal governor of Massachusetts Province, regarded loyalty to the king as his first responsibility. He insisted that the tea be brought ashore and the disputed tax, in the form of an import duty, be paid in full.

That's when the "Mohawks" hatched their secret plan to destroy the tea.

Everyone knew there was going to be trouble when the merchant ship *Dartmouth*, carrying 114 chests of fine blended tea, sailed into Boston Harbor on November 28, 1773.

Handbills nailed to trees and posted on fences all over town proclaimed: "Friends! Brethren! Countrymen! That worst of plagues, the detested TEA . . . is now arrived in this harbor."

An emergency town meeting was called for November 29, the day after the *Dartmouth* arrived. By nine o'clock that morning, so many people had showed up that they could not squeeze into Faneuil Hall, where town meetings were usually held. The crowd moved over to Old South Church, Boston's biggest auditorium. It was big enough to hold most of the five or six thousand angry colonists who had come from miles around to protest that day.

5

The meeting voted unanimously to block any attempt to bring the tea ashore. The colonists agreed that they would refuse to pay the hated tea tax, imposed by a remote and distant British Parliament. They demanded that the tea be shipped back to England, tax unpaid.

Armed volunteers were recruited to go down to the harbor and guard the *Dartmouth* until it left port. The ship's captain was warned that he would unload the tea only at his peril. Then the town meeting was adjourned amid shouts and applause.

Governor Hutchinson was not pleased. He had been appointed to his office by King George, and it was his duty to enforce the king's laws. When he was informed of the town meeting, he insisted that the *Dartmouth*'s tea be brought ashore and the tax paid in full.

When two more tea ships, the *Eleanor* and the *Beaver*, sailed into Boston, the governor ordered British warships to block the harbor. No ship would be allowed to leave without paying the tea tax.

Time was running out. Under the law, a ship had twenty days after reaching port to unload its cargo and pay any taxes, or to sail away. Once twenty days had passed, the ship's cargo had to be taxed. The *Dartmouth's* grace period would expire on Friday, December 17. Then the ship could be forcibly unloaded.

Another protest meeting was called for December 16, the day before the tax deadline. A cold rain was falling as a huge crowd from Boston and neighboring towns gathered again at Old South Church. This time there were more people than the church could hold—more than had ever before come together at one place in Boston. Those who could not find a seat or room to stand congregated outside, hanging around the church doors, hunched up against the raw, wet weather.

Inside the church, the colonists voted to make one last appeal to Governor Hutchinson. Francis Rotch, the young owner of the *Dartmouth*, was sent to ask the governor for a permit that would allow his ship to leave the harbor with the tea still in its hold.

Late that afternoon, as it was growing dark, the governor sent word that he would not back down.

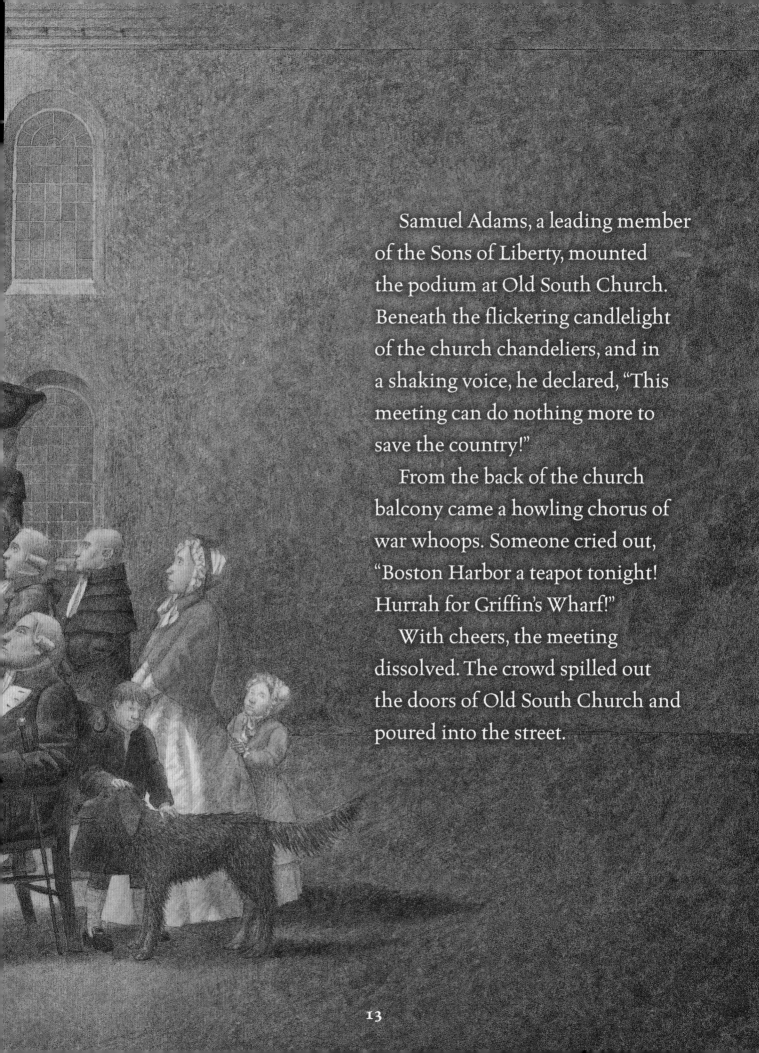

Samuel Adams, a leading member of the Sons of Liberty, mounted the podium at Old South Church. Beneath the flickering candlelight of the church chandeliers, and in a shaking voice, he declared, "This meeting can do nothing more to save the country!"

From the back of the church balcony came a howling chorus of war whoops. Someone cried out, "Boston Harbor a teapot tonight! Hurrah for Griffin's Wharf!"

With cheers, the meeting dissolved. The crowd spilled out the doors of Old South Church and poured into the street.

It was just before six o'clock. Night had fallen. The rain had stopped. A thin young moon was rising over Boston.

A bunch of men disguised as Mohawk Indians, carrying axes and hatchets, were hurrying down Milk Street toward the harbor, heading for Griffin's Wharf where the three tea ships were anchored. They had wrapped blankets around their heads and shoulders, and smeared their faces with coal dust, lampblack, and red paint. A growing crowd of people who had just left the church followed close behind. Everyone seemed to know that the "Mohawks" were actually fellow townsmen in disguise, though it was hard to identify any one of them.

Joseph Levering, who was a schoolboy at the time, remembered holding a whale-oil lantern high above his head as his father and several other men painted their faces earlier that day and admired one another's artistry.

Those disguised "Mohawks" were members of the Sons of Liberty. For several days, they had been making secret plans to destroy every pound of tea at Griffin's Wharf if the ships were not allowed to carry it away. Since they were running a great risk, they attempted to hide their true identities. If their names became known, they could be arrested and tried for destroying the property of the East India Company, the British firm that owned and imported the tea.

"To prevent discovery," recalled Joshua Wyeth, who was fifteen, "we agreed to . . . resemble Indians as much as possible, smearing our faces with grease, lampblack or soot, and should not have known each other except by our voices. Our most intimate friends among the spectators had not the least knowledge of us. We surely resembled devils from the bottomless pit rather than men."

Some of those men were well-known citizens, members of prominent Boston families. Others were tradesmen and artisans—blacksmiths, carpenters, printers, masons, and shipwrights. They were united by their shared conviction that the British tea tax was a threat to their liberties.

As the "Mohawks" converged on Griffin's Wharf, hundreds of other people were gathering at the waterfront to watch or even join in the action. Some were young apprentices attracted by the shouts and war whoops in the streets who joined the party on the spur of the moment.

Peter Slater, a fourteen-year-old rope maker's apprentice, was the youngest person to take part in the destruction of the tea. His employer, suspecting that there might be trouble in Boston that night, had locked Peter in the boy's upstairs bedroom. When Peter heard the uproar in the street, he put his rope-making skills to the test. He knotted his bedding together, hung it out the window, slid down to the street, and ran off to join the fun.

Nineteen-year-old Samuel Sprague, a mason's apprentice, was on his way to a date with the girl he would later marry when "I met some lads hurrying along towards Griffin's Wharf, who told me there was something going on there. I joined them, and on reaching the wharf found the 'Indians' busy with the tea chests.

"Wishing to have my share of the fun, I looked about for the means of disguising myself. Spying a low building with a stovepipe . . . I climbed the roof and obtained a quantity of soot, with which I blackened my face.

"Joining the party, I recognized among them Mr. Etheridge, my [employer]. We worked together, but neither of us ever afterwards alluded to each other's share in the proceedings."

The crowd swept down Milk Street, swerved into Hutchinson Street, and quickly reached Griffin's Wharf. The *Dartmouth* and the *Eleanor*, each with 114 chests of tea in its hold, were tied up alongside the wharf. The *Beaver*, with 112 chests, was nearby.

Alexander Hodgdon, a mate on the *Dartmouth*, had watched the crowd coming. In his eyes, it seemed like an awful lot of people. "Between six and seven o'clock this evening, came down to the wharf a body of about *one thousand people*," he wrote in the ship's log, carefully underlining the most important facts. "Among them were a number *dressed and whooping like Indians*. They came on board the ship, and, after warning myself and the custom-house officers to get out of the way, they [opened] the hatches and went down into the hold" where the tea was stored.

Joshua Wyeth recalled: "Our leader, in a very stern and reasonable manner, ordered the captain and crew to open the hatchways and hand us the hoisting tackle and ropes, assuring them that no harm was intended them. The captain asked what we intended to do. Our leader told him that we were going to unload the tea, and ordered him and his crew below. They instantly obeyed."

As the "Indians" went to work, they welcomed reinforcements from the rapidly growing crowd of onlookers. "Everything was as light as day, by means of lamps and torches," Robert Sessions remembered. "A pin might be seen lying on the wharf."

Sessions, who had been twenty-one at the time, impulsively went aboard one of the ships "and took hold with my own hands. . . . The chests were drawn up by a tackle—one man bringing them forward [in the hold], another putting a rope around them, and others hoisting them to the deck and carrying them to the vessel's side. The chests were then opened, the tea emptied over the side, and the chests thrown overboard."

The men and boys on the ships worked and the crowd on the wharf watched in silence, "no clamor, no talking," Sessions recalled. "Nothing was meddled with but the tea on board." The only sounds were the *whack-whack-whack* of the axes and hatchets breaking open the tea chests, and the splashing of water. "I never worked harder in my life," Joshua Wyeth remembered.

Because the water was at low tide—only two or three feet deep along Griffin's Wharf—the tea thrown overboard began to pile up like stacks of hay. Some of the apprentices jumped overboard and waded through the chilly December water, using shovels to scatter the tea more widely.

After all the tea had been dumped, the ships' decks were swept clean. Everything was put back into its proper place. Then a ship's officer was asked to come up on deck from his cabin to see that no damage had been done, except to the tea.

By nine o'clock, less than three hours after the first "Indians" had boarded the ships, the work was finished. And though British troops were stationed nearby and His Majesty's warships rode at anchor in the harbor, no one had attempted to interfere with the destruction of the tea. With hundreds of onlookers crowding the wharf, British authorities did not dare risk a violent confrontation. "I could easily have prevented the execution of this plan," Admiral John Montagu explained in his report the following day, "but must have endangered the lives of many innocent people by firing upon the town."

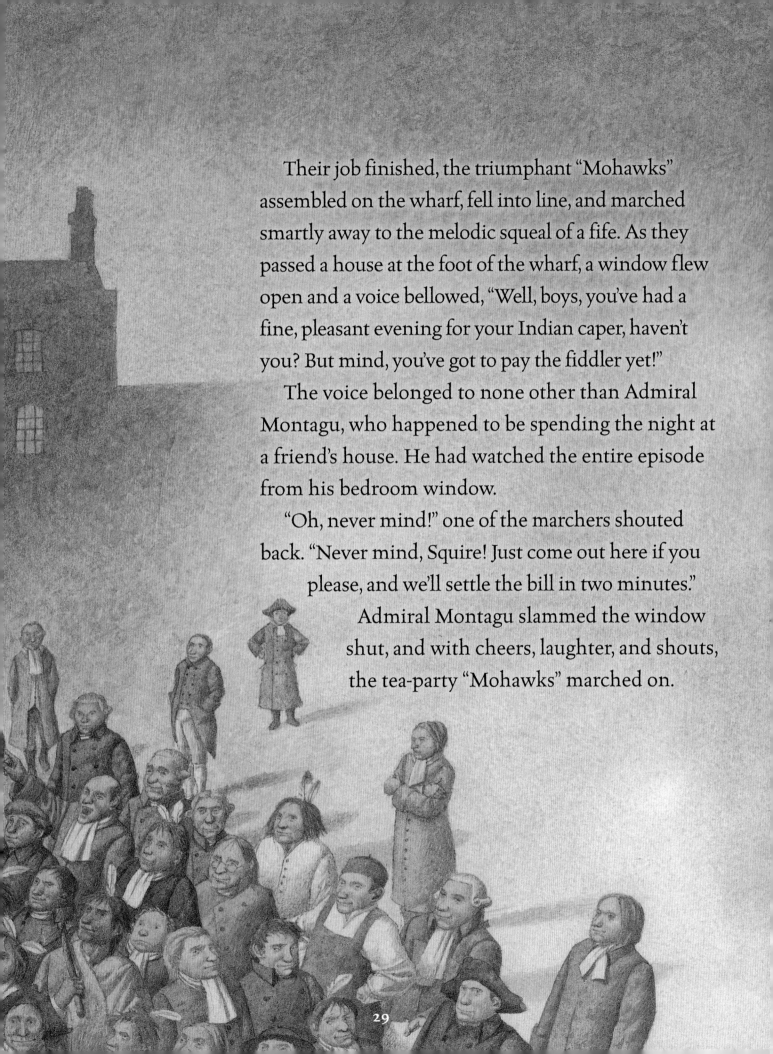

Their job finished, the triumphant "Mohawks" assembled on the wharf, fell into line, and marched smartly away to the melodic squeal of a fife. As they passed a house at the foot of the wharf, a window flew open and a voice bellowed, "Well, boys, you've had a fine, pleasant evening for your Indian caper, haven't you? But mind, you've got to pay the fiddler yet!"

The voice belonged to none other than Admiral Montagu, who happened to be spending the night at a friend's house. He had watched the entire episode from his bedroom window.

"Oh, never mind!" one of the marchers shouted back. "Never mind, Squire! Just come out here if you please, and we'll settle the bill in two minutes."

Admiral Montagu slammed the window shut, and with cheers, laughter, and shouts, the tea-party "Mohawks" marched on.

When one of the men got home that evening and took off his boots, some tea leaves fell out. According to family legend, he scooped them up and dropped them into a tiny bottle, which his family kept for generations as evidence that one of their ancestors, Thomas Melville (the future grandfather of the writer Herman Melville), had taken part in the great Boston Tea Party.

"The next day joy appeared in almost every countenance," reported the *Massachusetts Gazette*, "some on account of the destruction of the tea, others on account of the quietness with which it was effected."

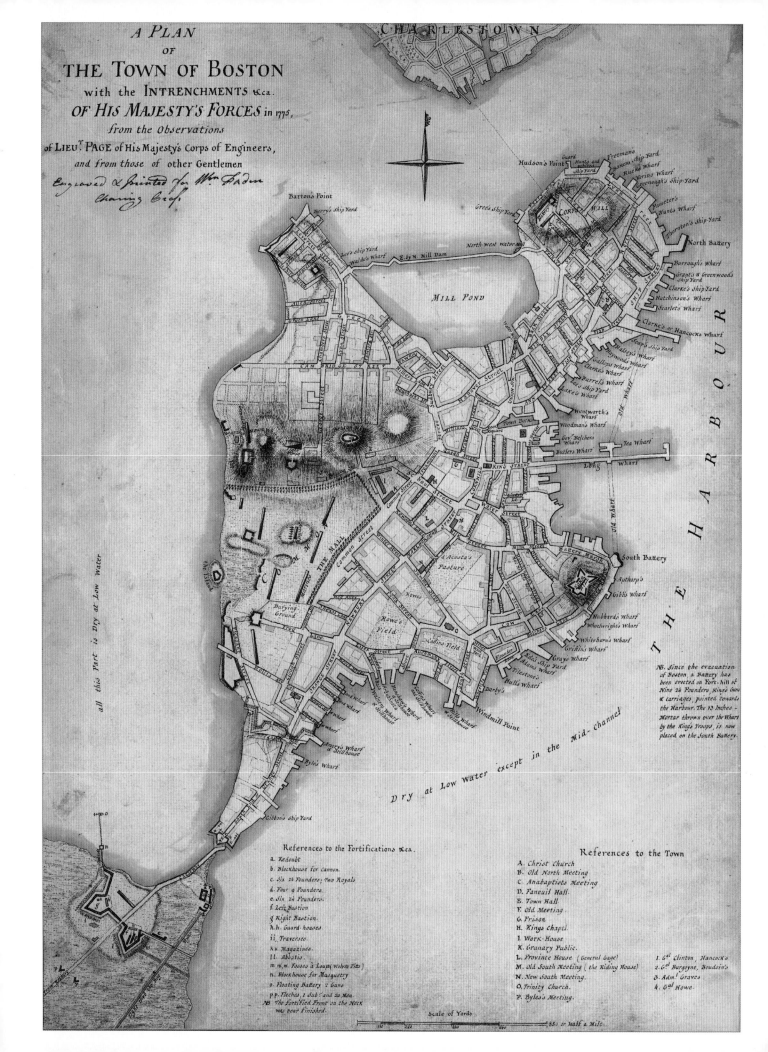